Rocky Flintstones Sweet Treats;

Compiler: Rocky Flintstone;

Editor and chief cook: Wilma Flintstone;

Assisted by Belinda Blumenthal, Bella Ridley et al;

Foreword;

Wilma, the Glee Team and I, have compiled this little recipe booklet to help bridge the gap between the slow lane and the fast lane.

Fast living city slickers and 90% of Belinkers still need to eat at home albeit now and again, or find they have to entertain... so this is our contribution to your life in the fast lane.... albeit generated in the slow lane....

Now, don't expect to find your chicken and chips, or steak and red wine sauce recipe here... no, it's all about the dessert...

the end to a fine meal where you just need a little something to make it perfect.

Or indeed you just need a massive pick me up at 11.00 am in the morning...

Or perhaps a little bit of love and send me to sleep happy at midnight.

jus sayin...

Table of Contents:

During his childhood whilst growing up on a farm in Ireland Rocky can remember many sweet treats. Whilst he had the usual gorgeous homemade biscuits and cakes there were other delicacies, known today as tray bakes. These are a gooey mixture put into a tray, left to set and then cut into generous pieces. Bella just loves them especially because they don't need much cookin'... and Belinda agrees so much with Bella that they've installed a microwave in Belinda's office. Well, Belinda had the budget and Bella knew how to plug it in...

Snacks were a part of daily living on a farm and as children Rocky and his brothers were always hungry. Everyone had to work physically hard outside on the farm which sharpened the appetite. They would of course have the traditional three meals a day; Breakfast was at 8am; Dinner (lunch) at 1pm, this being the main meal of the day, and Tea (dinner) at 6pm. However, to fortify these meals they would also have snacks at set times. Belinda and the Glee team just so love this concept and they coerced Rocky and Wilma into writing all the best recipes down in this book! It meant they only had to go to the Pentra after work.

Enjoy!!!

Ingredients;

Now Belinda and Bella would agree with Wilma that all the ingredients can be substituted if you can't get the exact ones. The recipes are pretty easy and you can practise with the simple ones (just mix ingredients together with no cooking) first…. Bella is ace at this already!

When you advance to cooking, you'll bake most of the recipes in a moderate oven which is Gas mark 4 or 180 degrees centigrade in the UK and Europe and 350 degrees Fahrenheit in the USA and elsewhere…. the Glee team are so multi-cultural it begs to ask the question why are Steeles Pots and Pans not sponsoring this book???????

OK…you'll know your own oven… or microwave…. and they all vary, so just watch with greater attention the first time you use the recipe and correct the timings as necessary… Belinda is used to disappointments so don't be put off by failure the first time around… Bella just presses more buttons and turns more knobs hoping it all works….

Equipment.

Oven and hob;

Microwave;

Large bowl;

Pie dish;

Baking trays;

Large spoon;

Measuring jug;

<u>Basic ingredients;</u>

Flour; Some recipes have SR or Self Raising flour but you can use plain flour and a measure of baking powder if you do not have SR flour; Giselle prefers to add her own Baking Powder as she likes a fast raiser... but we couldn't comment on this.

Golden syrup; Bella also likes this on porridge... go figure...

Butter or margarine; Use the hard versions of these, not the spreadable ones as they work better when cooking; Belinda agrees whilst Bella likes to work at the hardening process... a glutton for punishment.

Unless you are making a plain cake margarine is usually fine; Yuuggghhhh says the Glee Team.

Sugar and castor sugar; the only real difference between them is one of fineness, castor sugar is finer; and used exclusively for dusting, a bit like Jim Sterling's wedding cake decorations.

Brown sugar; it's sugar, it's brown and used in high end coffee shops... have it with high tea... sorry coffee in Claridges.

Eggs; The Duchess uses free range exclusively... but she has a coop.

Lemon flavouring is the flavour Rocky was used to but you can use orange just as easily; (which he now prefers... but don't quote him on that...)

You can alter all the flavourings as long as the consistency is the same;

For example; cherries for nuts;

If the consistency is not right just add a little milk, slowly, slowly; or vice versa.....

These are the basics which you will need to keep in stock.... in your larder... beside your little black book... you know, where you keep Des Martin's limo service number.

You'll need the ingredients below for certain recipes;

Coconut;

Dried fruit;

Cherries; (In Ireland they use glace cherries which are cherries preserved in syrup, sometimes dried fruit as well. This is because fresh ones were hard to come by.)

Cornflakes;

Cocoa or drinking chocolate; Children and Bella prefer drinking chocolate as it is sweeter but cocoa is fine... Belinda and Giselle are both into cocoa;

Ground almonds and other nuts; Obviously a "no-no" for nut allergy sufferers. We think Bill in HR is in this bracket.

Dried fruit;

Condensed milk;

Digestive biscuits or plain biscuits; Substitute Grahams crackers or Maria cookies in the US or wherever you can find a Sterling Corp store.

Heavy cream;

Chocolate;

Coffee essence;

Vanilla essence;

Lemon Juice;

Orange Juice;

Evaporated milk;

Gelatine;

Sherry;

Cottage cheese;

Milk;

Irish Whiskey or Rum; but don't tell the Glee Team you have it in stock.

Jelly or Jello;

Apples;

Ginger;

Vinegar;

Cream of tartar;

Peanuts; again be careful with nut allergy sufferers;

Dates; the fruit, not what the Glee Team do each evening.

Apricots;

Short crust pastry;

Icing sugar;

Jam/Jelly;

Marshmallows;

Chapter 1

Tray Bakes;

These are made with no cooking... even Rocky can make these.... If you listen carefully you can hear Wilma and Belinda laughing in the background....

A tray bake means a sweet treat that has been put into a shallow rectangular metal cooking tray after mixing or cooking to set. It can then be cut into pieces, stored in a Tupperware container... Belinda's favourite and served at your convenience. These bakes play a very big part in the sweets tradition of Ireland. Even James Spooner who is Scottish adores them and serves them whenever anyone pops in.

No cooking means no oven cooking; the ingredients are melted on the hob in a pan or in a microwave and then the dry ingredients added.

These are simple to do and taste delicious!... even Des can do this!!!!

Rocky's Crunch;

Belinda smacked her lips,

'Hey Bella... this is super easy to make, pass the syrup!!'

'Belinda, you are a saucy one.... and a cook as well! Can I have that spare Mars Bar?'

Ingredients;

1 tablespoon of golden syrup;

2ozs (50gms) of butter or margarine;

2 large Mars Bars chopped into large chunks;

Cornflakes or other cereals; We use cornflakes but it is a matter of taste!

Method;

Melt the syrup, butter and Mars bars first in a microwave or on a hob.

If using the hob stir constantly.

If in the microwave take out and stir every 30 seconds or so.

Do not over heat or it will burn.

When the ingredients are melted and mixed, stir in the cornflakes.

Put the mixture onto a lightly greased or lined tin with silicon or greaseproof paper and leave to set.

Cut into smallish pieces when cool as it is very rich.

This can make a great birthday cake.

Make it bigger by doubling up the ingredients and shape the melted mixture into the number of the age of the birthday boy or girl!

'OK Belinda, now it's my turn,' said Bella, 'we're going to make my......'

Bella's Surprise Snowballs;

Ingredients;

15 marshmallows;

15 digestives biscuits; Substitute Grahams crackers or Maria cookies in the US

1 small tin of condensed milk;

Desiccated coconut;

Method;

Crush the biscuits and add the condensed milk.

Cover the marshmallows in the mixture and then roll each one making a round ball.

Roll the balls in the coconut.

'That's it Belinda, no cooking, just mixing...' said Bella proudly.

'Yum, yum in my tum!' replied Belinda licking her lips..... but Bella... snowballs?... I never knew you were frigid?

'My softies are the best,' Giselle scoffed… 'so easy to make and Tony just adores them!'

Giselles Softies; aka Marshmallow Rolls;… did someone say her surname?

Ingredients;

15 marshmallows;

15 digestives biscuits; Substitute Grahams crackers or Maria cookies in the US

1 small tin of condensed milk;

Desiccated Coconut;

2ozs (50gms) glace (preserved in syrup) cherries;

Method;

Crush the biscuits;

Cut the marshmallows into four;

Chop/dice the cherries;

Mix all together and add the condensed milk;

Make into a long log and roll over the coconut.

Wrap in greaseproof paper and chill in the fridge until firm.

Store in a cool place and slice as required.

'Wowser… Giselle, I never took you for a softie…' said Bella licking her fingers.

Belinda Blinked;

'Belinda darling... I do sooo love apricots, it's a pity Lord Clarence and Sir James aren't here to help us eat them!' said a purring Duchess.

The Duchess's Balls; aka Apricot Balls;

Ingredients;

8ozs (200gms) dried apricots;

Half a cup of desiccated coconut;

1 small tin of condensed milk;

Half a cup of soft brown sugar;

Grated rind of an orange;

Method;

Mix all the ingredients together and leave to stand for an hour;

Take one teaspoon of mixture at a time and roll into a ball and coat with the coconut.

An easy way to do this is to put the desiccated coconut in a plastic bag.

Put in a few balls at a time and toss them in the coconut filled bag.

Keep in the refrigerator or in a sealed tin or Tupperware.

Belinda thought for a moment... 'You know that old saying My Lady, when you've got them by the balls, their hearts will follow...'

The Duchess coughed.

'I just love a good cheese cake Belinda... soft on the top and hard on the bottom... my idea of a real cook!' James Spooner licked his lips in anticipation.

Spooner's Cheese Cake;

Ingredients for the base;

8 digestive biscuits crushed; Substitute Grahams crackers or Maria cookies in the US

2ozs (50gms) melted butter/margarine;

2 desert spoons of castor sugar.

Method for the base;

Mix these together and put into a greased loose bottomed (push out base) deep baking tin;

Ingredients for the topping;

1 small can of Carnation milk, Whipped up;

1 lemon jello/jelly made up;

1 lemon;

8ozs (200gms) of cream cheese;

Half a cup of sugar;

Method for the topping;

Cream the cheese and sugar;

Add the juice of the lemon;

Make the jello/jelly and leave to cool;

When cold add to the whipped Carnation milk;

Add the cheese mixture and a few drops of vanilla essence and mix well;

Spread onto the base and place in the fridge;

Serve with cream as a pudding or cut into small pieces and serve as a tray bake.

'But James,' Belinda answered, 'I thought you were a more of a cheese and biscuits man?'

Sweets…. made by only using the hob or microwave.

Des Martin's Bonfire toffee;

Ingredients;

16ozs (450gms) of soft brown sugar;

4ozs (100gms)of butter;

1 tablespoon of vinegar;

4 tablespoons of golden syrup;

Method;

Put all the ingredients in a heavy pan and bring to the boil stirring slowly all the time;

Boil for about 20 minutes and put into a greased tin to set;

Be careful as this mixture is very hot and will burn if splashed;

Des sighed, he did love a fireworks party.

Ken Dewsbury's Regular Toffee;

Ingredients;

1 large tin of condensed milk;

5ozs (140gms) of sugar;

3ozs (90gms) of margarine;

1 tablespoon of golden syrup;

A few drops of vanilla essence;

Method;

Melt the margarine and add the sugar, condensed milk and golden syrup;

Boil slowly in a heavy pan for 15 minutes;

Make sure you are stirring continuously;

Test for when it is ready by dropping a small amount into cold water;

If it sets it is done;

Add the vanilla essence and allow to set;

Ken chewed and chewed and chewed, then sucked his teeth, 'Aye, that were reet good Belinda… fancy a tour round my cellar?'

Chapter 2

Tray bakes to cook in the oven;

These are slightly more time consuming than the "no oven cooked sweets" but are still very easy. Rocky is wary of this method of cooking. Belinda feels it brings out the chef in her whilst Wilma smiles and gets on with it.

Jim Stirling's Toffee shortbread;

A firm favourite! don't skimp on the portions…. Jim likes a monster bit.

Ingredients;

4ozs (120gms) butter;

5ozs (140gms) plain flour;

2ozs (50gms) castor sugar;

Method;

Rub together;

Bake in a moderate oven Gas mark 4 180C 350F for 25 minutes;

Allow to cool and make the topping;

Topping ingredients;

4ozs (120gms) butter;

4ozs (120gms) soft brown sugar;

2 tablespoons syrup;

1 small tin of condensed milk;

Few drops of vanilla essence;

Method;

Melt the ingredients and bring to the boil.

Stir well for 7 minutes and add the essence;

This will be very hot so be careful;

Beat until thick and spread over the shortbread;

When cool top with melted chocolate;

Cut into small piece as it is very rich;

'Gee Belinder, I hope you like my home cookin... it makes a great dessert to a Steak, Ass and Tits BBQ...'

Hazel's Coconut Macaroons;

Ingredients;

1 small tin of condensed milk;

8ozs (225gms) coconut;

A drop of vanilla essence;

Method;

Mix the ingredients together and roll into small balls.

Bake in a moderate oven at gas 4 180C 350F for about 10 minutes;

Hazel has one before every time she flies... 'They're sooo light and airy.. I feel as if I'm floating in a balloon!'

'Yuugghhh...' Belinda replies, 'I so hate balloons.'

Peter Rouse's Porridge Oat Fingers; ... no lickin....

Ingredients;

6 tablespoons of porridge oats;

2 table spoons of self-raising flour;

3 tablespoons of sugar;

4ozs (120gms) of margarine;

Method;

Mix dry ingredients;

Melt the margarine and pour over the dry ingredients;

Mix well;

Spread onto an oven tray;

Bake in a slow oven at Gas mark 3 160C 325F for 45 minutes or until golden brown;

Cut into fingers whilst still hot;

Leave in the tin to cool;

'Hey Christina... do you think Belinda would like these next time she's over?

'Only if you cover them in mud and drawn on her naked ass Darling.' replied Chris.

Mistress Sweetjuices Paradise fingers;

Ingredients;

5ozs (140gms) chocolate;

4ozs (120gms) desiccated coconut;

2ozs (50gms) chopped cherries;

4oz (120gms) of caster sugar;

1 egg;

Method;

Melt the chocolate in a microwave or over a bowl of hot water;

Put into an oblong or square baking tray;

Unusually the chocolate will be your base;

Mix the other ingredients;

Spread the mixture over the chocolate;

Bake at Gas mark 4 180C 350F or in a moderate oven for 20 minutes;

'Great night club food.' Belinda remarked as she left the Moulin Marron.

Tony Sylvester's Biscuits;

Ingredients;

6ozs (170gms) of margarine;

6ozs (170gms) of flour;

3ozs (80gms) of sugar;

Vanilla essence drops;

Method;

Cream the margarine and sugar by beating together;

Add the flour;

Mix with a few drops of vanilla essence thrown in;

Roll into small balls;

Bake for 15 minutes in a moderate oven at Gas mark 4 180C 350F;

To vary the flavour, add chocolate powder or cocoa powder, or even desiccated coconut to the flour before mixing.

Soo Tony Sylvesterish... boring, basic but brilliant...

'Not the 4B's Belinda...? jus askin...

Alfonse Stirbacker's Quick Shortbread;

Ingredients;

9ozs (250gms) of plain flour;

3ozs (80gms) of corn flour;

4ozs (120gms) of castor sugar;

Mix these ingredients together;

Melt 4ozs (120gms) of margarine with 4oz (120gms) of butter;

Add to the dry ingredients and mix;

Press into a shallow oven tray;

Bake in a moderate oven Gas mark 4 180C 350F for about 45 minutes;

Cut into fingers whilst still warm and leave to cool;

'Well Belinda,' Bella remarked, 'very Quick, very Alphonse...'

'And totally Belgian.' Belinda replied.

Wolfgang Bisch's Afgans; seriously Germanish….

Ingredients;

6ozs (170gms) of butter;

6ozs (170gms) of margarine;

4ozs (120gms) of castor sugar;

5ozs (140gms) of plain flour;

Crushed cornflakes;

Vanilla essence drops;

Method;

Cream by beating together the fats and sugar;

Add sifted flour and a few drops of vanilla essence;

Roll into balls and then roll in the crushed cornflakes.

Bake in a moderate oven Gas mark 4 180C 350F for 15 minutes.

'Yah… zeese are ze best Afgans in ze world… baked in my pots und pans, you vill not be dizzapointed!'

Belinda yawned.

Prof Prof Slinz's daily Bread;

Ingredients;

8ozs (225gms) of plain flour;

3ozs (80gms) of sugar;

3oz (80gms) of butter;

Half teaspoon of baking powder (bicarbonate of soda);

1 beaten egg;

1 tablespoon of milk;

Method;

Rub butter into flour;

Add sugar and baking powder;

Add the beaten egg and milk;

Mix;

Roll out thinly;

Cut into rounds;

Bake in a moderate oven Gas mark 4 180C 350F for 10 minutes;

Bella snorted, 'Prof Prof… yeah, well at least we've got the blueprints for this recipe written down.'

Giselle scowled and ate another piece.

Belinda Blinked;

"God Nodded" Biscuits;

Ingredients;

8ozs (225gms) of plain flour;

4ozs (120gms) of butter;

4oz (120gms) of caster sugar;

1 beaten egg;

Half teaspoon of baking powder;

Half teaspoon of lemon rind or to taste;

Method;

Rub butter into the flour;

Stir in the sugar;

Add the lemon rind and baking powder;

Add the beaten egg;

Mix thoroughly;

Roll out to a quarter of an inch depth;

Cut with cutters;

Bake in a moderate oven Gas mark 4 180C 350F for 20 minutes;

Sprinkle sugar over all when out of the oven;

Leave to cool;

'Dearest God, I think your biscuits are the money tits...' Belinda thought as she chomped her way through her fourth.

God nodded;

Maeve's Almond Horn Cookies... Tony adores them;

Ingredients;

8oz (225gms) of butter;

2 cups of flour;

Half a cup of icing sugar;

4ozs (120gms) of ground almonds;

Half a teaspoon of almond flavouring;

Method;

Cream the butter and sugar; (beat it together).

Add almonds flour and flavourings;

Form into horn shapes;

Bake in a moderate oven Gas mark 4 180C 350F for 15 minutes;

Cover in icing sugar when out of the oven;

Leave to cool;

'Belinda,' Bella said worriedly, 'should we be eating these... I mean... Tony really loves them...'

'Don't worry Bella... we can always hit the Pentra later...'

Jailmans Sweet Oatcakes;

Ingredients;

2 cups of oats;

1 cup of sugar;

1 cup of plain flour;

1 cup of desiccated coconut;

Half a cup of butter;

2 cups of peanuts;

1 desert spoon of syrup;

1 desert spoon of milk;

1 teaspoon of baking powder;

Method;

Mix the butter and syrup;

Add baking powder and milk;

Mix the dry ingredients together;

Add to the mix;

It should be stiff, if not add more oats... slowly;

Put in a greased tin;

Bake in a moderate oven Gas mark 4 180C 350F for 30 minutes;

Cut into squares when cool;

Note there are nuts in this recipe!

Jailman has these every time he gets a new contract, it's his way of saying thank you to the gift that keeps giving...

'Bella... so that was what he was eating when we were in the clink?

Bella screams 'Aaaarrrrggghhhhhh!' as the memories come hurtling back to her....

Hank Skank's Coffee Walnut Biscuits;

Ingredients;

4oz (120gms) of butter;

2ozs (50gms) of castor sugar;

4ozs (120gms) of plain flour;

2ozs (50gms) of chopped walnuts;

2 teaspoons of instant coffee powder;

Method;

Cream the butter and sugar by beating together;

Add the dry ingredients;

Using a teaspoon put dollops onto a baking tray.

Bake in a moderate oven Gas mark 4 180C 350F for 20 minutes;

Note there are nuts in this recipe!

Jim Sterling grunted, 'Gee Belinder, at least he can't spread them all over you and lick them off...'

'You think Jim??'

Belinda Blinked;

Belinda Blumenthal's Crunch;

Ingredients;

8ozs (225gms) of margarine;

5ozs (140gms) of castor sugar;

3ozs (80gms) of desiccated coconut;

3ozs (80gms) of crushed cornflakes;

1 tablespoon of cocoa powder;

5ozs (140gms) of self-raising flour;

Bar of chocolate;

Method;

Melt the margarine;

Stir in the other ingredients adding the flour last;

Bake in a moderate oven Gas mark 4 180C 350F for 30 minutes;

When cool cover with melted chocolate;

'More upmarket than Rocky's Crunch Belinda...' Bella noted as she ate her fifth piece...

'Well Bella... good shout... you see that's what's wrong with Rocky... he just doesn't understand the world of business...'

'Belinda... pass the Chards... hic...'

Patrick O'Hamlin's Almond Fingers;

Ingredients;

2ozs (50gms) of butter;

2ozs (50gms) of ground almonds;

1 egg yolk;

2ozs (50gms) of sugar;

4ozs (120gms) of flour;

Milk;

Method;

Rub butter into the flour;

Add the sugar and ground almonds;

Add the egg yolk; (save the white for later).

Add enough milk and mix to make a stiff paste;

Roll out and put in a greased tin;

Topping Ingredients;

1oz (30gms) of icing sugar;

White of an egg;

3ozs (80gms) of chopped almonds;

Method;

Whip the white of the egg until stiff;

Add icing sugar and chopped almonds;

Spread on to the pastry;

Sprinkle heavily with sugar;

Bake in a moderate oven Gas mark 4 180C 350F for 20 minutes;

Cut into fingers whilst it is hot;

Note there are nuts in this recipe!

Ken Dewsbury groaned…. 'Not more bloody almonds… Patrick…'

Des Martin smiled… 'Just lick the fingers Ken… and pretend it's the Boss!'

Rocky's Chews;

Ingredients;

3ozs (80gms) of plain flour;

3ozs (80gms) of margarine;

5ozs (140gms) of castor sugar;

12ozs (340gms) of chopped dates;

4ozs (120gms) of chopped walnuts;

2 eggs;

Method;

Cream the margarine and sugar by beating together;

Add the beaten eggs;

Then mix in the flour;

Add the fruit and nuts;

Spread into a greased oven tin;

Bake in a moderate oven Gas mark 4 180C 350F until firm for about 30 minutes;

Cut into pieces;

'Belinda!' shouted Giselle and Bella... 'are these for his dog?'

Paddy the Barman made a mental note. 'Don't serve chews to the Glee Team...'

Belinda's Paradise Cake;

Ingredients;

The Base;

4ozs (120gms) of short crust pastry;

A tin of jam of a flavour you like…. perhaps strawberry;

The Filling;

4ozs (120gms) of margarine;

4ozs (120gms) of castor sugar;

2ozs (50gms) of chopped cherries;

2ozs (50gms) of chopped walnuts;

1 tablespoon of sultanas;

2 tablespoons of ground rice;

2 tablespoons of ground almonds;

2 eggs;

Method for the Base;

Line a baking tin with the pastry;

Spread with the jam;

Method for the Filling;

Cream the margarine and sugar by beating together;

Add the beaten eggs and mix;

Add the rest of the ingredients adding a little milk if the mixture is too stiff.

Spread over the jam and bake in a moderate oven Gas mark 4 180C 350F for 30 minutes;

Dust with sugar when cold;

Note there are nuts in this recipe!

James Spooner sighed... 'Ahh, paradise... if only...'

Belinda Blinked;

Chapter 3

Cakes;

Cakes in Ireland are usually iced to make them all the sweeter or served with cream; All these recipes will require baking in the oven;

Cristina Rouse's Lemon Cake;

Ingredients;

4ozs (120gms) of soft margarine;

6ozs (170gms) of self-raising flour;

6ozs (170gms) of castor sugar;

4 table spoons of milk;

2 large eggs;

Grated rind of 1 lemon;

Method;

Cream the margarine and sugar by beating together;

Add the eggs and the other ingredients;

Add the milk last as you need to get a soft dropping consistency;

Put in a cake tin and bake in a moderate oven Gas mark 4 180C 350F for 40 minutes.

When just out of the oven mix 3 table spoons of icing sugar with the juice of a lemon;

Pierce the top of the cake several times with a skewer and drop on the lemon juice sugar;

'Ohhh Christina,' mouthed Belinda, 'this is the cows moo...!'

'Well Belinda, you can kiss my ass...'

Petra's Almond Sponge;

Ingredients;

4ozs (120gms) of margarine;

4ozs (120gms) of sugar;

2 eggs;

2ozs (50gms) of self-raising flour;

2ozs (50gms) of ground almonds;

Method;

Beat the margarine and sugar together;

Add the beaten eggs;

Add in the flour and ground almonds;

Mix thoroughly;

Bake for 40 minutes in a moderate oven Gas mark 4 180C 350F;

Note there are nuts in this recipe!

'Not more bloody almonds…' shouted Ken Dewsbury.

'Yah!' replied Petra.

Helga's Chantilly Sponge;

Ingredients;

6ozs (170gms) of margarine;

6ozs (170gms) of self-raising flour;

6ozs (170gms) of castor sugar;

1oz (30gms) of ground almonds;

1 teaspoon of vanilla essence;

3 eggs;

2ozs (50gms) of red glace cherries; (cherries preserved in syrup)

2ozs (50gms) green glace cherries;

2ozs (50gms) of walnuts;

Method;

Cream the margarine and sugar by beating together;

Add essences;

Beat in the eggs;

Stir in the other ingredients;

Bake in a loaf tin in a moderate oven Gas mark 4 180C 350F for about 1 hour;

Note there are nuts in this recipe!

'But… but… Helga,' Belinda spluttered, 'I thought you were based in Holland… not France or should I say, Chantilly?'

'Je parle Francais also my petite goose…'

Madame Chocolats; Chocolate Layer Cake; ... because this is what life is all about...

Ingredients;

7ozs (200gms) of self-raising flour;

8ozs (225gms) of castor sugar;

Pinch of salt;

1 tin of evaporated milk;

2 tablespoons of drinking chocolate, cocoa makes a sweeter cake;

Method for the cake;

Rub the margarine into the flour and salt;

Stir in the beaten eggs with 5 tablespoons of evaporated milk, and water if needed to get a soft consistency;

Add the vanilla essence;

Beat well;

Put into a cake tin and bake in a moderate oven Gas mark 4 180C 350F for 35 minutes;

Take out and leave to cool;

When cool cut in half across the middle.... Not down the middle;

Ingredients for the Filling;

4ozs (120gms) of butter;

6ozs (170gms) of icing sugar;

2 tablespoons of cocoa or drinking chocolate;

A little milk;

Few drops vanilla essence;

Method for the Filling;

Beat all the ingredients together until thick;

Spread onto both halves of the cake just like a sandwich;

Put the cake halves together;

Spread more filling on top;

Decorate with chocolate sprinkles;

The Duchess smiled and rolled over feeling complete. 'That was a stunning cake Belinda, where did you learn to make it?'

'Belgium.' Belinda replied licking her fingers excitedly.

Jim Thompson's Gingerbread;

Ingredients;

4ozs (120gms) of plain flour;

Pinch of salt;

2 teaspoons of ground ginger;

Half a teaspoon of bicarbonate of soda;

2 tablespoons of oil;

2ozs (50gms) of soft brown sugar;

2ozs (50gms) of treacle;

2ozs (50gms) of syrup;

1 egg;

3 tablespoons of milk;

Method;

Mix the flour, salt, ginger and bicarbonate of soda;

Add the syrup and treacle;

Add the other ingredients;

Beat until smooth;

Pour into a square tin;

Cook in a moderate oven Gas mark 4 180C 350F for 20 minutes;

Cut into squares;

'Jim... that was delicious.' Bella exclaimed.

'Gorgeous Jim.' Giselle cried.

'Now, get us to the Pentra... quick... that pool car will do!' added Belinda.

Bella's Fruit Cake… beware… it's full of nuts….

Ingredients;

5ozs (140gms) of self-raising flour;

5ozs (140gms) of butter;

3ozs (80gms) of sugar;

8ozs (225gms) of mixed dried fruit;

1oz (30gms) of cherries;

2oz (50gms) of ground almonds;

Half a teaspoon of cinnamon spice;

2 eggs;

Method;

Beat the fat and sugar together;

Add the eggs and beat further;

Add the flour and fruit and beat in;

If the mix is a bit dry add some flour and water;

Bake in a slow oven gas mark 3 160C 325F for 2 hours;

Note there are nuts in this recipe!

'Bella,' Giselle queried, 'I didn't think you liked nuts…'

'Only the small round kind Giselle.'

Belinda Blinked;

Chapter 4

Puddings;

You will find some traditional and not so traditional recipes here;

Grigor's Syllabub;

Ingredients;

Juice of 1 lemon;

3ozs (80gms) of castor sugar;

1 glass of sherry;

Half a pint of double/heavy cream;

Method;

Whip the cream until stiff;

Mix the lemon juice, sugar and sherry;

Fold in the cream;

Put in the refrigerator to set in the dishes you will serve to the table.

Grigor sobbed, 'Belinda, it reminds me so much of mother Russia.'

Belinda helped herself to another dollop.

Georgie Porgies Chocolate Rum Pie;

Ingredients;

Base;

One 8 inch (65cm) cooked short crust pastry case.

Filling;

1 and a half ounces (40gms) of butter;

3 tablespoons of plain flour;

1 and a half cups of milk;

3 table spoons of sugar;

3ozs (80gms) grated chocolate or chocolate chips;

1 teaspoon of coffee essence;

A few drops of vanilla essence;

2 eggs;

Rum to taste;

Method;

Melt the butter in a pan;

Add flour and cook for 2 minutes;

Stir in the milk, add sugar and chocolate with the coffee essence;

Stir until it boils;

Then stir in the egg yolks;

Do not boil!!!

Add vanilla essence and the rum to taste;

Put into the pastry case and chill until set.

Decorate with cream;

'Georgie Porgie,

Pudding and Rum Pie,

Kissed the girls and made them cry,

And then he turned evil and got into knife crime...

Bisch Blinked;

Chiara Montague's Pavlova; ... terribly posh... but so good....

Ingredients;

3 egg whites;

1 teacup of castor sugar;

1 teaspoon of wine vinegar;

1 teaspoon of vanilla essence;

Meringue Method;

Beat the 3 egg whites until stiff;

Beat in the sugar, vinegar and vanilla;

Cover the baking tray with baking paper and put the meringue on this making a round hollow shape;

Cook in a slow oven Gas mark 3 160C 325F for about 1 hour;

When done leave to cool;

Peel off the baking paper and then fill the meringue with fruit and whipped cream;

Decorate as desired;

'Chiara!' Belinda squeaked, 'the Duchess is coming to dinner, what can we have after the Chicken Kiev... something classy..?

'I know,' Chiara nodded violently, 'my terribly posh pavlova... all the aristos love it...'

Belinda Blinked;

Paddy the Barman's Irish Whiskey Coffee Pie;

A big favourite in Ireland and on the Rocky wish list;

Ingredients;

Packet of vanilla whip desert;

2 teaspoons of instant coffee powder;

Half a cup of cold milk;

3 tablespoons of Irish whiskey…. No other type will work!

Half a cup of heavy cream;

One baked 8 inch (60 cm) pastry case base;

Method;

Mix the vanilla whip desert mix with coffee, add the milk and beat;

Blend in the Irish whiskey…. No tasting!

Beat the cream until thick and fold into the mix;

Fold all onto the pastry case base and leave to set;

Decorate with cream.

This is a great pudding for St Patrick's Day!

Belinda went to the Pentra Bar.

'Ms Belinda,' Paddy the Barman asked, 'what can I get you?'

'Ohh Paddddyyyy…. I'd looove a piece of your Irish Whiskey Coffee Pie?'

Paddy the Barman Blinked;

Cosmo Macaroon's Vanilla Ice Cream;

Ingredients;

Quarter pint of double/heavy cream;

4 table spoons of icing sugar;

2 egg whites;

Vanilla essence;

Method;

Whip the cream and add the icing sugar;

Add the vanilla essence;

Beat the egg whites until stiff and fold in;

Pour into a plastic container and freeze;

'You see, Belinda, this dish is an essential part of our summer vacation down here in Oz.' Cosmo paused as Belinda tasted it.

'Mmmmm Cosmo... cream, vanilla, egg whites... Oh... a little taste of plastic container!!!'

Macaroon Blinked;

Marco Ouriquez's Pineapple Soufflé;

Ingredients;

1 small tin of pineapple crush or pieces;

1 lemon jello/jelly;

1x 6oz (170gms) tin of Carnation milk;

Method;

Mix the fruit juice and water to make the jello/jelly;

Cool;

Beat in the Carnation milk;

Add the pineapple pieces and leave to set;

'We grow all the best pineapples in Brasil... and God knows it...' Marco smiled.

Belinda Blinked;

Dave Wilcox's RSM Raspberry Cheese Flan;

Ingredients;

Base;

One 8 inch (60cm) short crust cooked pastry case base;

Topping;

3ozs (80gms) cream cheese;

1 tablespoon of milk;

Raspberry jelly/jello mix;

Boiling water;

1 small tin of raspberries;

One cup/carton of double or heavy cream;

Method;

Beat the cream cheese and milk until it is smooth;

Spread over the pastry case base;

Make the jello/jelly with the boiling water;

Add the raspberries;

When the mixture is starting to set spread it over the cream base;

Serve with whipped cream on top;

'Raspberries Dave,' Belinda said incredulously… 'you actually go out and pick raspberries?'

'Yes Boss.'

'Well fuck me…'

Contessa Lucia's Lemon Cream Flan;

Base Ingredients;

4ozs (120gms) of Digestive or Ginger biscuits; Substitute Grahams crackers or Maria cookies in the US

2ozs (50gms) of melted butter;

Base method;

Make the base by mixing the digestive or ginger biscuits with the melted butter;

Substitute Grahams crackers or Maria cookies in the US

Put the mixture in the bottom of a flan dish and leave to set;

Filling Ingredients;

One Quarter pint of double/heavy cream;

6oz (170gms) can of condensed milk;

2 large lemons;

Filling method;

Mix the lemon rind with the condensed milk and cream;

Add the juice of the 2 lemons;

Pour onto the base and chill;

Serve decorated with cream;

'James... I do love a flan... make me that one Contessa Lucia does....'

'Is that the Lemon Cream or... the Orange Cream, Belinda?'

'Why not strawberry... the summer fruit?

Spoons Blinked;

Des Martin's Lemon Curd;

Ingredients;

2 lemons;

2ozs (50gms) of butter;

2 eggs;

8ozs (225gms) of sugar;

Method;

Beat the eggs and put them in a bowl with the butter and sugar;

Add grated lemon juice and rind;

Heat slowly by putting the bowl over a pan of hot water;

Cook until it thickens;

'Lemon Curd Des... are you joking?' an upset Chiara Montague protested.

Des Martin Blinked;

Sir James's Lemon Meringue Pie;

Ingredients;

8 inch (60 cm) pastry case

Lemon curd mix;

Meringue mix;

Method;

Fill a pastry case with the lemon curd;

Top with the meringue mix in a wave style;

Bake in a hot oven Gas mark 8 240C 460F for 20 minutes or until the meringue tips are browned;

'Hrrmmppphhh... eat it... it's fucking good!'

All the COCK members licked their plates.

Giselle's Apple Tart;

Ingredients;

One 8 inch (60cm) pastry case base;

6 apples;

 4ozs (120gms) of sugar;

One carton of cream or custard;

Cooked Apples Method;

Peel and core apples;

Slice and cook in a little water with the sugar until soft;

Add water if too much boils off;

Adjust the sugar to taste;

Tart Method;

Line the bottom of a pie dish with pastry or use a premade pastry case;

Fill with the mixture of cooked apples;

Top with a pastry lid;

Bake in a moderate oven Gas mark 4 180C 50F for 25 minutes;

Serve with cream or custard;

At Halloween it is the Irish custom to add small coins well wrapped in grease proof paper into the apple mixture. A clever cook will ensure each slice of pie will have a coin. Do not serve with cream or custard. Make sure you warn your guests to expect a "solid bite" when enjoying their "Halloween" apple tart. Great fun but serve with caution!

'Well Belinda...' noted Bella, 'it takes one to know one...'

Giselle Blinked;

Chapter 5

Loaves and Breads;

Soda bread is the bread of Ireland;

Rocky was brought up with the wheaten bread variety, but you can also make it with white bread.

It is easy to make but does not keep, so unless you can eat it all that day... or the next, freeze it!

Rocky's Irish Soda Bread;

Ingredients;

3lbs (1.4kg) of wheat meal flour;

1 teaspoon of salt;

3 heaped teaspoons of baking powder;

3ozs (75gms)of butter;

2 beaten eggs;

1 and half pints of sour milk... buttermilk;

Method;

Rub butter into the dry ingredients;

Add eggs and the baking soda;

Mix thoroughly;

Bake in a hot oven gas mark 8 240C 460F for 30 minutes and then in a slow oven Gas mark 3 160C 325F for the final 15 minutes;

'This tastes nice Bella.'

'Hmmm, not bad Belinda.'

'You guys are sooo sycophantic...' Giselle scoffed.

Blumenthal Walnut Bread;

Ingredients;

4 cups of plain flour;

1 cup of sugar;

A quarter cup of chopped walnuts;

4 teaspoons of baking powder (bicarbonate of soda);

1 teaspoon of salt;

1 egg;

2 cups of milk;

Method;

Mix the dry ingredients;

Make a well in the centre of this mix;

Add a beaten egg and the milk;

Mix together thoroughly;

Bake in two small greased loaf tins for about 40 minutes in a moderate oven Gas mark 4 180C 350F or until firm;

Mother Blumenthal's home recipe, kept in the family over the ages.

'Not more bloody nuts.' Ken Dewsbury exclaimed.

The Youngish Man's Tea Break;

Ingredients;

1 cup of mixed fruit;

1 cup brown sugar;

1 cup of cold tea…. Yes cold tea!

2 cups of self-raising flour;

1 beaten egg;

Method;

Soak the mixed fruit, brown sugar and cold tea all mixed together overnight.

Mix the flour and beaten egg together;

Add the overnight mixture and thoroughly mix;

Divide into 2 small loaf tins and cook for 40 minutes in a moderate oven Gas mark 4 180C 350F;

Every active Manager needs a tea break, and this is Sam's… enjoy!

Alfie's Fruit Loaf;

Ingredients;

1 cup of currants;

1 cup of sugar;

1 cup of raisins;

1 cup of water;

2 cups of self-raising flour;

1 egg;

Method;

Put the fruit and water in a saucepan;

Boil for 5 minutes;

Allow to cool;

Add the egg and flour;

Mix well;

Grease 2 small loaf tins and bake for 40 minutes in a moderate oven Gas mark 4 180C 350F;

'Well Belinda…. I like a fruity loaf,' said Bella… 'and this one suits me down to the ground… measure me up Alfie!!!'

Alfie Blinked;

Steeles Pots and Pans Scones;

Ingredients;

4 cups of self-raising flour

A pinch of salt;

2 ozs (50 g) of butter or margarine;

One cup (300ml) of milk;

Method;

Preheat the oven to Very Hot or Gas mark 9 250C 475F;

Mix the flour and salt;

Rub in the fat until it looks like bread crumbs using your finger tips;

Add the milk slowly mixing with a fork;

Stop when it makes a ball, do not make it too wet;

Turn onto a surface covered in flour and roll out to a depth of one quarter of an inch (0.5cm);

Cut with pastry cutters;

Put on a baking sheet and cook for 10 minutes in the preheated oven above;

Leave to cool but serve warm;

Cut into two and spread with jam and thick cream or butter;

You can add dried fruit of any sort to this recipe;

You can also add cheese to make a savoury snack;

These really need to be eaten hot;

Note; sweet scones will keep a day but if you are not eating them immediately then freeze!

Only to be cooked with Steeles Pots and Pans hardware... anything else risks failure... do not, repeat, do not use the Tri Oxy Brillo range for this product. You have been warned.

James Spooner's Scotch Pancakes;

These were a staple food and were cooked on the griddle of the old cast iron cooker.

Ingredients;

1 cup milk;

1 cup of flour;

Half a teaspoon of baking powder;

1 egg;

Method;

Sift the flour and baking powder together;

Beat the egg and mix with the milk;

Add to the flour;

Whisk it all together;

Heat a griddle or a heavy frying pan;

Add a little butter to melt and then pour it over the pan;

Add the batter in spoon fills to the hot pan;

When bubbles form turn the batter over;

Keep them warm as you cook until you have used all your mixture;

Serve warm with butter, golden syrup or jam;

Try flipping them out of the pan onto the plate!

These pancakes are really good James.'

Spoons smiled and answered, 'It's my mother's recipe Belinda...'

'Great.' Belinda answered.

Rocky's Potato Bread;

This was a staple of Rocky's childhood, and still is…. most Saturday mornings!

It is always served with a traditional Irish cooked breakfast or as Rocky would say an Ulster Fry of bacon, fried egg…. maybe two? sausages, mushrooms, fried bread, fried potato bread….. and a milky tea.

When he was a child his mother made it most mornings using the left over potatoes from the day before.

Ingredients;

Pre-cooked and mashed potatoes;

Flour;

Pinch of salt;

Method;

Take the left over mashed potatoes and add a little flour and salt;

Mix thoroughly;

Heat a griddle and cook like a pancake until brown on each side;

The best result comes from cooking them with the bacon and egg as they absorb the bacon fat and taste delicious!

'The only way,

to start the day.'

Belinda Blinked;

<u>Conclusion;</u>

Wilma and I hope you have enjoyed these recipes from Ireland, some dating back over 80 years. Many are ones we still make today. They're all handed down so are not totally precise; therein lies the charm as you can adapt them to suit your own needs and your family size. This is what Rocky's home cooking is all about.

All the birthday cakes we made for our children over the years were a choice between Madam Chocolat's Chocolate Layer Cake, or Rockys Crunch... we had it last week for our 33 year old!

Every St Patrick's Day is also an excuse to once again sample the very fine Paddy the Barman's Irish Whiskey Toffee Pie.

Over the years we have also enjoyed the other recipes both at Granny's in Ireland or at our own family home.

Enjoy!

Rocky and Wilma Flintstone.

Ireland; January 2020

Return to Contents

Made in the USA
Monee, IL
28 November 2021

83311915R00056